The

Self-Mastery & Fulfillment Workbook

---

50 Exercises & Master Keys for Living Like You Mean it!

Antonia Martinez, Ph.D.

New York

Mystery School Books
a division of Conscious Enterprise, Inc.
New York, NY

If you are unable to order this book from your local bookseller, you may order it online.

www.SelfMasteryCamp.com

ISBN 978-0-9717939-2-7
Printed in the United States of America on acid-free paper.

To Celeste Harper, my first teacher on this path, thank you for opening my soul. This book is a direct result of your presence in my life.

Table of Contents

You are about to evolve. You are about to close the chasm between who you are and who you are meant to be.

Author's Note

This work is dedicated to the enlightenment of Humankind so every soul might come to see its own spiritual brilliance. The *Self-Mastery & Fulfillment Workbook* was written with the intention to help you embrace the authentic power within and use it consciously to move toward your destiny. The contents of the book represent an important collection of wisdom teachings, mystical insights, and spiritual guidance acquired during my first twelve years of meditation, spiritual training, and metaphysical study. I share with you the same guidance that has motivated me, inspired me, and impacted my well-being and spiritual growth. This wisdom has touched me in a most profound way and given me the energy and spiritual substance to pave and walk my own path. It can do the same for you.

~Antonia Martinez

"Live a little!" That's what people sometimes say to encourage a sheltered, stuck-in-a-rut, timid or unjustifiably cautious friend to let go, loosen up and dare to do something different. Intuitively, they know that life is about feeling alive. What makes you come alive? I mean, *really* alive, organically from within, not artificially. Do you know? If you do know, are you doing it often? Are you living your life like you mean to be more alive each day for the rest of your life? Or are you living like you've gotten as good as you'll ever get? Imagine what it might mean for you to master the art of being alive...and being yourself in a completely fulfilling way.

Perhaps for you it will mean enjoying the freedom, success, or love that you've been looking for. Perhaps it will mean greater happiness and well-being. Or maybe it will mean developing the confidence, courage or character that you wish you had. Whatever it means for you, the road to self-mastery begins with a personal shift—one that breaks down the internal barriers that block you from becoming the kind of man, woman, lover, leader, parent, entrepreneur, artist, politician, student, teacher...human being...that you intend to be. It means fearlessly seizing opportunities to create a life that you're truly excited about living. This is what the *Self-Mastery & Fulfillment Workbook* and the online courses will help you achieve.

Mastering yourself may seem easier said than done. The road to self-fulfillment can be littered in some places with personal roadblocks. A roadblock, however, is like a shadow puppet; it is a distorted projection of something you perceive to be bigger and more powerful than it really is only because of the light in which you see it and yourself. Change your self-image, change your perception, and you change the apparent power an obstacle has over you. Revolutionizing the way you define yourself and approach your life is your first step in the *Self-Mastery & Fulfillment Workbook*.

You may not know it (or perhaps you do know it but are reluctant to embrace it) but, there is something about you that is brilliant and awe-inspiring. This "something" is the seed of your success and prosperity in life. It is the root of the legacy you will cultivate and leave behind. When you stop hiding it, judging it, fearing it, squandering it or holding it back, you begin to shine. When you shine, you naturally and effortlessly excel and inspire growth all around you in everything you do and everyone you meet. The *Self-Mastery & Fulfillment Workbook* helps you overcome obstacles, blind spots, hang-ups, self-doubt and patterns of self-sabotage that obstruct your inner light so that you can uncover and command the presence, power, and artistry of being the real you.

Think about this for a moment: what most people know about themselves (or think they know about themselves) is obsolete. Their self-knowledge is based primarily on what they remember about the person they used to be yesterday, a week ago, six months ago, twenty years ago, or more. And some, unfortunately, have mostly second-hand knowledge (theories really) about themselves, constructed and passed on to them by friends, lovers, relatives, society, etc. Those theories and memories are but shadow images of the Self. Who you were yesterday is who you were yesterday. Today is a new day. You have the power to choose to be a different kind of person with a different destiny. The guidance and self-mastery exercises in this workbook help to lift you out of the roles, routines and life patterns in which you have become stuck so that you can connect with a more fluid, flexible and authentic sense of self. What follows is a gradual opening to possibilities that were previously unthinkable to you.

The workbook is divided into twelve sections or development paths, called Journeys, that deal with a variety of life issues, growth objectives, and personal and professional challenges. Each journey consists of one or more personal workshops to guide you through a focused and accelerated holistic process of development and self-mastery. To aid your development, the book features a holistic technique developed by the author called Inner Power Mapping™, which helps you to quickly experience the mental, emotional, physical and spiritual shifts that are essential in achieving inner fulfillment coupled with outer success. Your experience with this workbook will be unique because it is interactive and shaped by your personal experiences. The exercises have a cumulative effect on your growth process. Each empowers you to make choices and take action that more effectively, meaningfully, and accurately reflect the person you are truly meant to be. The training and exercises in this workbook and the online courses at www.SelfMasteryCamp.com can help you to:

- Discover and embrace your power, potential and gifts.
- Know your worth, clarify your values and live your vision.
- Maintain your balance and focus, even while under stress.
- Redirect negative energy into self-liberating choices.
- Assert your personal power in a balanced way.
- Break cycles of stagnation and underachievement.
- Face and break free from your fears and self-doubts.
- Build confidence, courage and self-esteem.
- Cultivate trust and respect between yourself and others.
- Be decisive, disciplined and in control of yourself.
- Live purposefully and experience fulfillment.
- Connect with your innermost Self and deepest passions.
- Stop hiding from yourself and your power.
- Manage your emotions and your mind.
- Handle change gracefully.
- Stop procrastinating and wasting time.
- Uncover and change self-defeating patterns.
- Understand and improve your relationships.
- Approach life more creatively, openly, and spontaneously.
- Take effective action, especially in situations where you have been timid or non-committal.
- Regain your balance and direction after getting off track.
- Recognize what's not working in your life and what to do about it.
- Commit to yourself and your life path with certainty and enthusiasm.

The Inner Power Mapping Technique & the Holistic Approach to Self-Mastery

The holistic approach to self-mastery takes the whole person into account as an interactive system of mental, physical, spiritual, and emotional and energies. Each affects all the others because they are essentially different sides of the same coin, rather than four separate energies. To create permanent change in your life, that change must penetrate all fours sides of yourself, so to speak. This is called integration, meaning that the change becomes a natural part of your whole being, not just a fake skin you're trying to wear. When it's real, every part of you from your cells to your ideas resonates with the new you.

Mind, body, spirit and emotions must all be in sync with the new tune you are trying to play on the instrument called your life. If any one of them is off key, your tune falls flat, despite your having played the right musical pattern. If you've ever found yourself doing "all the right things" but getting all the wrong results, then something within you is out of tune. The Inner Power Mapping Technique™ aids the internal tuning process, allowing you to quickly pinpoint your most discordant energies in a given situation (the "real problem") and resolve them. Because it taps the creative mind, the technique minimizes the mental strain usually associated with this kind of work and turns it into a creative and dynamic process of self-discovery. It is also an extremely valuable technique for those who are uncomfortable about, unable, or unwilling to express themselves verbally or in writing.

Many people have been taught to take a generally one-sided approach to bringing balance to their lives, focusing primarily on the psychological, intellectual or material aspect of a problem. As a result, their success (if there be any) tends to be lopsided and impermanent. A particular problem may appear to be resolved, yet in other areas the person continues to flounder. Why? Because they have only treated an outer symptom of the real problem, which is a much deeper issue at the root of several seemingly unrelated difficulties, that has yet to be discovered and addressed.

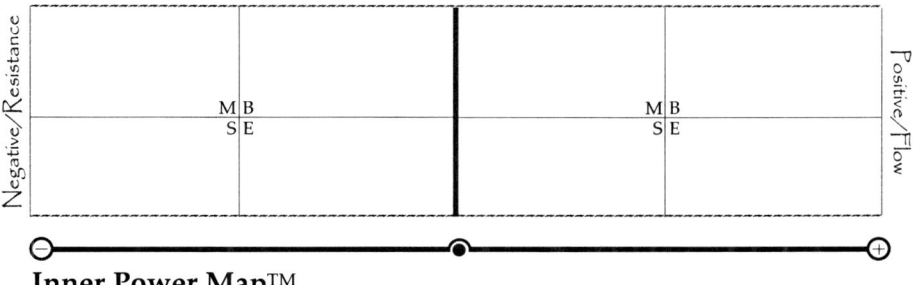

Inner Power Map™

   With the Inner Power Map™ , you can more accurately assess your use (or misuse) of power, and how best to bring your life into alignment. Combined with the other activities that comprise each personal workshop, the map helps you get to the root of whatever is creating conflict between your internal desire and your external experience. You are then able to draw your own personal road map that shows you the way from challenge to change.

   The map consists of two main hemispheres. The left or negative side is used to pinpoint detrimental or resistant energy in the mind, body, spirit or emotions that surface when you encounter a challenge. The right or positive side is used to pinpoint advantageous or motivating energies that can help you overcome your weaknesses and reach your growth objective. Both hemispheres consist of four quadrants representing negative and positive spaces in your mind, body, spirit and emotions. By observing how those spaces interact, you can begin to see a chain reaction of attitudes and behaviors that are triggered when certain issues are faced. Your strongest and weakest energies are the key to breaking the chain. By using the balance beam at the bottom of the map along its length, you can determine how to find and maintain the personal balance and equilibrium that will restore order to your life and create the conditions for optimal growth. For detailed instructions on using the map and technique, see page 18.

A journal is the soul's notebook. A place where the power of the pen, the word, awareness and intention meet for the unified purpose of educating and unfolding the Self. When kept consciously, a journal becomes an interactive and dynamic vehicle for incubating your selfhood and humanity.

On the surface it may appear that keeping a journal is automatically a conscious process. You're writing about your experiences and articulating your thoughts and feelings about them. But from a metaphysical point of view, archiving and memorializing your experience on paper is not in itself a conscious activity. What transforms journaling into a conscious and meditative process is its use as a catalyst for life change.

If you have kept a journal for any length of time, look back over the years. Have the names and places all changed while your status quo remained virtually the same? Have you written about the same things, had the same thoughts, the same ups and downs over and over again? Have you vented your frustrations within the safe confines of a journal page while conveniently never confronting the issue directly in your everyday life? Have you been very creative, journaling about many different things without much of it making a difference in your life? If your answers is yes to any of these questions, your experience with this workbook will help take your journaling (and your life) to a new level.

Practiced consciously with introspection and purpose, journaling is a powerful tool for mastering mind, body and emotions, and becoming attuned to spirit. It is a path for discovering personal truth and examining how best to demonstrate it in your experience.The *Self-Mastery & Fulfillment Workbook* introduces both the new and experienced journal keeper to a holistic journaling approach that stimulates organic growth and simultaneously transforms your inner and outer life.

The foundation of every journey is its beginning. Did you start at the "Beginning..." (page 3) or did you skip it? Did you skim through it quickly without paying close attention to the message or did you take it to heart? How many false starts have you experienced in your life because you bypassed the crucial beginning stages or lacked a fundamental piece of knowledge that would have made all the difference? Getting off to a proper start is the first step in this process. "Beginning the Shift to Self-Mastery" preps your mind for the work you are about to do and the metamorphosis you will undergo. Like a first impression, the first step can influence the entire course of events that follows. If you've bypassed the "Beginning..." of this workbook, if you've bypassed the beginning of anything else in your life recently or have gotten off to a rocky start, then begin again. Build a proper foundation for walking a new path.

The *Self-Mastery & Fulfillment Workbook* and online courses take you on a series of twelve developmental journeys. Each teaches a key holistic/metaphysical principle or concept that, once applied, lets you transform yourself the way you desire in all the "layers" of your life simultaneously.

Journey I: "Your Personal Renaissance" (Master Keys 1 - 22)

Your first journey in the workbook is "Your Personal Renaissance". It consists of twenty-two exercises and master keys that can produce significant shifts in your life. Your journeywork here helps you distinguish your authentic self from your "scripted" self. The scripted self is the you that thinks, says, feels, and does everything it's been conditioned to. It never deviates from the script—not even to experience fulfillment.

When people say, *"So tell me about yourself,"* your scripted self is who you talk about when you tell your story. Maybe the story starts with what you do for a living or the kind of family you come from. Whatever the details, the more of them people know, the more they think they know you. But the story of yourself and the authentic reality of yourself are two completely different things. Very few people know themselves outside of the story they tell. This journey propels you to get to know yourself outside of your story. It is only by moving beyond the script of your life story that you are free to move toward your destiny.

Journey II: "Your Goal in Life" (Master Key 23)

"What were you thinking?" Have you ever asked anyone that? Has anyone ever asked you that in the wake of some disaster that could have been foreseen and avoided? Right now there are millions of people who are consciously or unconsciously moving away from their goals in life and waiting for the end—the end of the year, the end of their career, the end of their marriage, the end of the road, the end of some particular chapter in their story, the end of their life—before doing anything to change their life's direction. Are you one of those people? Are you so distracted by your outer achievements or setbacks that you remain oblivious to what's happening within and around you as you obsess over them? Although hindsight may sometimes be 20/20, the truth is, by the time you look back, what's done is done. If, however, you can gain insight into the present moment, you will enjoy the creative power and immediate satisfaction of making the most of it. Your journeywork through "Your Goal in Life" can lead to important insights about your life goals, choices, and what they can create for you right now.

Choices make the world go 'round because they commit our thoughts, energy, and attention in one direction or the other. Every choice you make—to lie, to tell the truth, to go, to stay, to apologize, to keep quiet, to smile, to frown, to sleep, to stay awake, to punish, to forgive—commits your life to one direction or another. It is in the choosing that life really happens. While some choices may be difficult or unpleasant, if you are deliberate about making appropriate choices in the moment, then you can also be at peace in the moment with how your life is going. The exercise and master key for this journey empowers you to choose authentic goals that bring immediate peace to your life.

Journey III: "Your Essential Nature" (Master Key 24)

Do you know the story of *The Little Engine That Could*? A train hauling toys and other things to boys and girls anxiously awaiting on the other side of a mountain suddenly breaks down. Several big trains pass by offering one excuse after another for not stopping to help. Finally, along comes the Little Engine. Small though it was, and seemingly incapable of pulling the broken-down train full of toys over the mountain, the Little Engine chooses to call upon its inner strength rather than be hindered by its apparent limitations. "*I think I can, I think I can, I think I can,*" it tells itself as it struggles to the mountaintop. As it finally reaches the peak and starts to run effortlessly down the other side toward its destination, the Little Engine praises itself, "*I knew I could, I knew I could, I knew I could.*" The journey to "Your Essential Nature" is the journey of *The Little Spirit That Could*—the spirit that could envision its potential and rise to a challenge; that could think beyond its apparent limitations and dare to achieve the impossible; that could motivate itself to reach the mountaintop and run toward its destiny. That spirit, of course, is you.

No matter how much you ignore or deny the inner strength of your spirit, it is still there within you anyway. When you resist it, you merely weaken your ability to use it effectively and favorably in your life. The exercise and master key for this journey will help open you up to your true potential for greatness—if you let it!

Journey IV: "Conquering the Mind of Doubt" (Master Key 25)

The truth hurts. That's what we've been told. So when doubt enters your mind about why someone did what they did, or why this thing or that did or did not happen for you, the tendency is to gravitate toward ignorant bliss rather than investigate the truth. You gravitate toward ignorance when you're afraid of what you might learn if you start asking serious questions. Knowledge of the truth often breeds responsibility. You gravitate toward ignorance when you're afraid of what you may have to confront—what you'll have to be responsible for—once the truth is revealed. You run from the truth when you're terrified it will make a negative or humiliating statement about you. Contrary to popular belief, truth does not hurt. What hurts is the judgment you make about yourself and others based on the truth. Judgments perpetuate doubt, fear, and confusion. They do nothing to transform the situation. Judgments cloud the path to destiny and authentic self-fulfillment. Your journeywork in "Conquering the Mind of Doubt" helps to clear the cloud.

Journey V: "Your Energetic Bottom Line" (Master Keys 26 & 27)

Whatever personal gain you may acquire in life, how profitable is it really if you overtax your mind, body, and emotions in the process of attaining it? If you invest time, money, and effort into things that are fleeting and insignificant, you will find the grandness of your life escaping you. You will find yourself losing hope, faith, energy, vitality, health, clarity, opportunity, respect, joy, support, friendship, love, and attention. You will find yourself losing your ground, losing your grip, losing your balance—losing yourself. To lose sight of what matters is to suffer quite a loss indeed.

Many people are running on empty—some without even knowing it—because the outer trappings and distractions of the material world temporarily mask the depletion of their inner resources. To journey successfully across "Your Energetic Bottom Line" is to replenish and multiply the authentic value of your life. The exercises and master keys for this journey help you inventory and wisely invest your vital energy and authentic power.

Journey VI: "Relationships"
(Master Keys 28 - 33)

Relationships with others have great impact on your sense of self. Relationships can offer an external view of your innermost thoughts about yourself—who you are, who you hope to be, who you're ready to be, who you're afraid to be, and what you're willing or unwilling to do about it. The responses, reactions, and interactions you experience in your outer relationships directly reflect the relationship issues you have with your innermost Self. Sometimes you unconsciously use relationships to distract you from the inner reality that needs attention. When you relate soul-to-soul rather than ego-to-ego, you can recognize and seize opportunities for mutual growth. Your journeywork in "Relationships" intensifies your collaborative and creative power to reach your destiny.

What you see in others, what attracts, repels, empowers or disempowers you when you relate to others, offers important insight into your own capacity for self-love and nurturing. True self-love and self-fulfillment are interdependent. The exercises and master keys for this journey help you distinguish true, soul-based love from that which passes for love in the ego's eyes.

Journey VII: "Diminishing Conflict, Ego & Stress"
(Master Keys 34 - 45)

Ego is the fabricated, surface identity we come to erroneously accept as Self. Over time it becomes a hardened shell of conditioned responses and views, and seeks endlessly to justify itself and remain unchanged. The ego is always on the lookout for a threat—some potential breach of inner security. When in doubt, ego assumes the worst and goes on the defensive to resist, protect, deny, enforce, judge, distract, isolate, divide, and conquer. A threatened ego is the number one cause of inner and outer conflict and stress. Your journeywork for "Diminishing Conflict, Ego & Stress" in your life will help you develop a new approach for dealing with common experiences in which you are most likely to get caught up in your ego and lose sight of yourself, what's real, what matters, and what works.

The ego is not a creative problem solver. It always does whatever it has always done. Ego leads to rigor mortis of the mind and emotions, eventually rendering you inflexible in your thoughts, perception, approach, character, and courses of action. When you diminish ego, you increase exponentially your identification with authentic Self and your ability to consciously interact with what's happening within and around you. The less ego you have, the easier it is to maintain equilibrium while life happens. The exercises and master keys help to prevent you from losing hold of yourself when the pressure is on. They can help you connect with the right choices and action that will bring peace, healing, resolution, and fulfillment in the heat of the moment.

Journey VIII: "Social Consciousness" (Master Key 46)

How much of what goes on in the world happens because of what people do? How much of it happens because of what other people don't do about it? If your individual thoughts create your personal reality (and they do), then understand that our collective thoughts create our social reality. Local and global events are the stage on which our collective thoughts are dramatized. The journey through "Social Consciousness" is an examination of your role in those dramas.

Dependency, complacency, apathy, and fear of rocking the boat are chronic problems in today's society. On this journey, you examine the line between where you end and where you allow society to take your place. You also examine how this affects your ability to live life to the fullest. Individual and collective fulfillment (and dissatisfaction), are reflected back to you through the outer reality. Your journeywork here helps you recognize the extent of your power and take your sense of purpose to a new level.

Journey IX: "What Must Be" (Master Key 47)

Sometimes a soul's gotta do what a soul's gotta do. The journey through "What Must Be" empowers you to do just that. What you experience up until this point in the process helps you gradually clear your consciousness of things that keep you from authentic self-fulfillment. You will see for yourself, however, that there are times when there simply is no time for anything other than instantaneous transformation. If you intend to live life like you mean it, then you must let yourself arrive at the moment when you stop crawling and choose to take a stand.

The journey through "What Must Be" is an important process in which you begin to mature into your real power. You press onward, go deeper, and make the changes that really matter without making excuses for yourself. You realize there is no excuse for not living the life you are meant because that's what you came here for. This journey offers very simple wisdom, yet it is difficult to stomach if you have grown accustomed to spinning your wheels and going through the motions when it comes to reaching your destiny. The exercise and master key for this journey challenge you to reach an important milestone: to stop stalling and go straight to your destiny.

Journey X: "Your Responsibility"
(Master Key 48)

How serious are you about living a fulfilling life from an authentic place of power, while moving consciously toward your destiny? After you have successfully journeyed the previous path of "What Must Be," you will have not only reached an important level of maturation, but you will have also started radiating your unique brilliance with increasing power and consistency. The journey through "Your Responsibility" puts you in touch with a deep and powerful level of inner authority, and urges you to accept full creative and spiritual responsibility for yourself. It is an empowering step that takes guts. In the earlier journey of "Your Essential Nature," you learn that you wield the power of the universe in everything you do. "Your Responsibility" urges you to be ready, able, and willing to wield that power deliberately for the highest good. The exercise and mastery key reveal how you sabotage and cheat yourself out of what is right, and allow you to finally get out of your own way.

Journey XI: "Desire"
(Master Key 49)

Who is in control of your life? Is it you or your mind? The real you is not your mind; neither is it your body nor your ego. When you permit the desires of your false self (the inauthentic self) to overwhelm you, you lose control, you lose momentum, and you lose your capacity to reach your destiny. The desire that manipulates you, the desire over which you relinquish control of yourself and the moment, does not lead to fulfillment. It cannot because only the authentic Self can experience fulfillment. The false self can only be pacified—until its next craving.

Although desire can drive you to action, uncontrolled desire can drive you over the edge. False, uncontrolled desire enslaves you and diverts you away from what is meaningful and real. You gravitate toward false desire when you seek distraction from something you don't want to address. Underneath false desire is an authentic need to fill a void or heal a wound. This journey takes you right into the void, which can only be filled with self-love, nurturing, and truth—things that restore you to the totality of yourself. Authentic self-restoration cannot be wished into being. It can only be brought about through clear intention and consistent focus. The exercise for this final step of the process leads you to a pivotal milestone that helps you fill the void, fulfill your authentic desires, and live the life you are meant.

Journey XII: "Your Divine Self-design"
(Master Key 50)

This unique journey is completely different for everyone who undertakes it. It puts the power of total self-mastery and fulfillment directly into your hands.

Each of the twelve developmental journeys in the *Self-Mastery & Fulfillment Workbook* consists of one or more personal workshops that coach you through an accelerated and holistic growth process in some area of your life. As a result, you're able to clearly identify and fearlessly take the next necessary step to get where you need to be. Personal workshops consist of five interactive activities that prepare you to make the self adjustment or life adjustment that will propel you toward your greatest possible success with the least amount of difficulty. The workshop activities are:

1. Contemplate the journey overview and master key.

2. Do the workshop exercise.

3. Use the Inner Power Map™ to assess and balance your negative and positive attitudes, energies, and patterns.

4. Write or draw on the 'Note to Self' journal page/workspace to reflect on or question your experience.

5. Complete the self-coaching worksheet.

Take workshops in sequence, or based on the Journey that fits your goal, or refer to the index to choose workshops based on a specific exercise or issue you want to work on. The following instructions describe how to use each activity for maximum benefit.

*Special note for groups and teams: Groups (such as study groups, sharing circles, or other gatherings of friends, colleagues, students or members) should follow the additional instructions that accompany each activity. Teams or workgroups functioning as a single unit should work collectively on each activity on behalf of the team. Teams should follow the special group instructions only if appropriate. Individual team members should subsequently use their personal self-mastery work to align themselves with the team's growth objectives.

Activity #1: Contemplate the journey overview and master key.
(Groups: read the overview and master key aloud, and then discuss.)

Immediately preceding each journey is an overview of its relevance to self-mastery and fulfillment. Read it before starting the journey. Contemplate how it applies to you. Next, read and contemplate the master key for the personal workshop you are doing. Master keys are words of wisdom and guidance composed of numbered verses. They help to unlock your mind and other closed doors standing in your way. You can focus on the entire text or only the most relevant verses.

Uncovering the deeper wisdom and power of a master key requires introspection. Wisdom cannot be reasoned or deduced. To grasp it, you must be willing to go beyond your mind and into your spiritual depth. The exercise that follows the master key will assist you in applying what you've learned.

Activity #2: Do the workshop exercise.
(Groups: share your individual results and experiences.)

There is a dimension of understanding that comes only from experience. The workshop exercise helps you to see for yourself the value of the key you are trying to master. Some exercises involve writing and some are activity-based while others require you to tap other resources to deepen your self-study. Each is an "experiment in consciousness" designed to guide you out of your habitual patterns and approaches so that you can be open to something new, more effective, and more fulfilling. Don't just go through the motions. Stay with an exercise until you get something out of it.

Activity #3: Use the Inner Power Map™ to assess and balance your negative and positive attitudes, energies, and patterns.
(Groups: use a large writing surface like a whiteboard or easel pad and work together to help at least a few members with their maps.)

The Inner Power Map™ appears opposite each master key. Throughout the workshop process, observe what you are experiencing internally and record anything significant on the map in the appropriate space for your mind (M), body (B), spirit (S) or emotions (E). Use keywords, metaphors and/or hand-drawn symbols to create a quick visual snapshot of what you're thinking and feeling (see a completed sample map on page 24). If applicable, consider your physical environment an extension of your body; the atmosphere, an extension of your emotions.

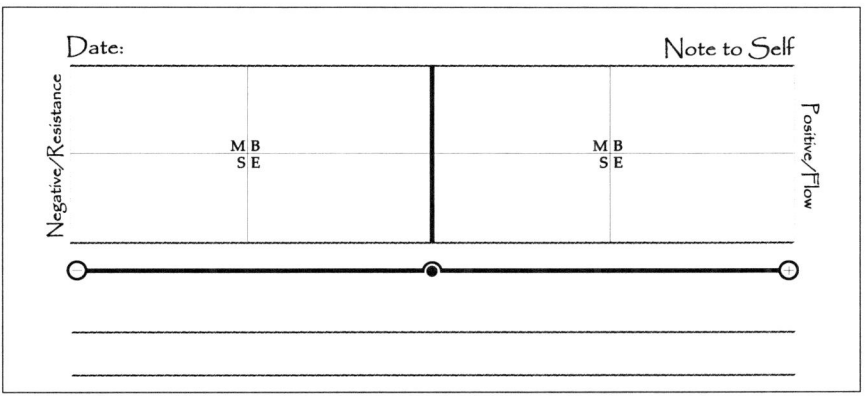

a. Pinpoint any negativity or resistance you experience on the left side of the map labeled Negative/Resistance. Spiritual negativity refers to difficulty with things of a spiritual nature, such as hope, faith, creativity, or character. Elaborate in the journal space if necessary. New insights may surface.

b. On the right side of the map labeled Positive/Flow, pinpoint the positive thoughts, feelings, or traits connected with your experience. Elaborate in the journal space if necessary. New insights may surface.

c. To begin the process of balancing and mastering your energy, first identify the negative energy on the map that feels "heaviest". Write it down on the negative end of the balance beam. This energy is the most disruptive and the one most in need of transformation if you are to grow. Examine how it triggers other energies on the map. Explore it further by journaling. You may discover something heavier that is really at work.

d. On the positive end of the balance beam, indicate the counter energy to the negative force. The counter energy may already be on your map. It may be the opposite of your negative energy but not necessarily. To discover it intuitively, use body language (miming, charades, etc.), metaphor, or symbolic imagery (visualization, doodling, etc.) to express the negative energy and then transform it into the desired positive state. For example, you might express the negative energy of depression with a mime, doodle or metaphor of being in a slump, and then transform or lighten up the heavy energy by redirecting it into "walking tall".

e. Identify the energy that will help you to more smoothly make the transition from the negative to the positive. The positive end of the balance beam tells you where to go. The energy at the center of the beam tells you how to get there. This is called the bridge or the bridging energy. Unless something suddenly clicks in your consciousness that enables you to quantum leap from one way of being to another (it can and does happen), the bridging energy will be your key to making the transition. To find it, use the same technique you used to find the positive end of the beam, but this time pay attention to the motivation behind your transformation. For instance, in the shift from slumping to walking tall, you might feel motivated by the idea of dressing the part, or a feeling of pride in your work. There are no wrong answers. Go with your gut. Journal in the workspace to help clarify and strengthen the bridging energy.

Activity #4: Write or draw on the 'Note to Self' journal page/workspace to reflect on or question your experience.
(Groups: encourage members to share their thoughts, feelings, insights or questions to stimulate group discussion.)

A blank journal page/workspace appears underneath each Inner Power Map™. Use it to record your thoughts, do your written exercises, and document your experience. Perhaps more importantly, use it to ask yourself any questions that arise during your process. Questions often reveal more than answers. Putting your thoughts on paper is also therapeutic. It can have the effect of "emptying your mind," thereby making room for new realizations. Also jot down any dreams that seem connected to your process.

Your journaling need not be polished or extensive. To be effective it must be legible and allow you to easily recall your experience, including relevant thoughts and feelings. A few notes are often sufficient (see page 25 for a sample journal entry). Enter the complete date when you make an entry; this will be invaluable when you want to assess your development later.

Activity #5: Complete the self-coaching worksheet.
(Groups: share your answers. Hold each other accountable for meeting deadlines. Follow up to share progress and results.)

Fill out the self-coaching worksheet that appears below each workshop exercise. You can use the journal page to gather your thoughts first. The worksheet will guide and pace you through your growth and development. It will provide structure and consistency throughout your process. The worksheet consists of seven key elements (see page 24 for a completed example):

Exercise: List and/or make a collage of seven very specific things you hope to do with your life—no matter how big or small.

My Message: ———————————————————————

My Creative Focus: ————————————————————

My Reluctance: ————————————————————————

---

1. **My Message:** What personal message does the master key and/or the exercise hold for you? My Message is where you

turn what you think you know into what you clearly understand and can apply in a real-life situation. There are no wrong answers. The goal is not to be right but to be clear. The message will influence how you approach your journeywork and any issue you are addressing.

2. **My Creative Focus:** Many people approach self-help and transformation by trying to fix what they think is wrong. The workbook's approach is to help you create what you feel is right. When you do, you naturally begin to uncreate the problem that got in your way—and you do so with considerably less effort than if you had focused on tackling it. This is because the problem you face is never really the problem. It is the result of the real problem you have yet to discover. By focusing on what you're inspired to create (your intention) you naturally "fix" the real problem without turning it into a battle against yourself. Your creative focus can also serve as a benchmark that you're striving for.

3. **My Reluctance:** Even when you are excited about creating something new in your life, you may sometimes feel reluctant to follow through on it for reasons you don't always understand. Once you start to venture beyond your limitations, you can sometimes feel the pull of your patterns and fears sucking you back in. What are you in the habit of doing, feeling, or thinking that blocks your way toward a more liberating choice? Acknowledge any reluctance you feel and record your thoughts and feelings on the journal page.

4. **My Willingness:** What commitment are you *willing* to make to yourself and your creative focus? Sometimes you're ready, able and willing to go all the way. Sometimes you're only willing to go so far. When it comes to transforming something in your life, what you "should" do is irrelevant if you're not willing to do it. Be honest in acknowledging what you're willing to do *right now*. That tells you where you are. Where you are is the only place you can start. It's the only place you

have any real footing or power. Make a clear and honest statement about your willingness to move forward.

5. **My Next Step:** Once you are clear about what you're willing to do, make a firm decision about what you'll actually do. Willingness can open up many possibilities but a decision will determine your course of action. State the action you will take to implement your creative focus. Stating your expected outcome can help you assess the appropriateness of your decision. Trial and error, however, is part of the growth process. Don't get too frustrated with yourself if you hit the occasional wall. Following your own advice may be the most challenging part of your process.

6. **My Deadline:** Talk is cheap. In the transformation process, realizations are soon forgotten and old habits quickly renewed when there is procrastination, lack of commitment to finishing the process, and a lack of accountability should you drop the proverbial ball. Once you've decided what your next step is, give yourself a maximum of thirty days to take it. Put it on your calendar so you don't forget.

Deadlines also make it obvious when you're serious about changing and when you're just playing games with yourself. If you're not ready to make a particular change, don't spin your wheels. Move on to something you're more willing to do. It is easy to get stuck between the fantasy and reality of change and not realize it until after you've wasted a lot of time. If you miss your deadline, it may be an indication that you need to adjust your pace, search your soul a little deeper for the right incentive or course of action, or be more realistic with your goals.

7. **My Results:** How well did you master yourself and the key you were working on? You make progress not merely by taking action, but by following through on *effective and relevant* choices. Indicate the most significant change you have experienced as a result of taking your next step.

Master Key 1

How does one begin the story of eternity? I say it begins with you. [2]Hope springs eternal and your best hope is always you. [3]You are the source of your own experience. This is the true story of yourself.

Exercise: List and/or make a collage of seven very specific things you hope to do with your life—no matter how big or small.

My Message: *Stop dreaming and get something done already! Focus on what you can do, not on what you wish you could.*

My Creative Focus: *To master the basics and best practices required for success in my 7 things. And be consistent.*

My Reluctance: *I feel a little overwhelmed by my own ideas. It's like, "oh, I have to learn all that?"*

My Willingness: *I'm willing to start with one thing right now - cleaning and decorating the apartment. I've avoided it for years!*

My Next Step: *Find tips, guidelines, etc. and make a list of the top 5 basic strategies for a clean, beautiful, organized home.*

My Deadline: *Sunday, July 22, 2007*

My Results: *Got the right shelves, tools, storage and accents for flair. I want company now. This is new. Deeper than I thought.* →

Negative/Resistance

Positive/Flow

going in circles mental static ◯ ∿∿	tense apprehension in stomach			
M B	S E		M B	S E
hopeless incapable	frustrated anxious	creative inspired		eager

○————————————●————————————⊕
incapable   excel at the basics   masterful

Workshop Exercise: My 7 things I hope to do

1. Start a successful media and publishing company

2. Open an alternative education school

3. Clean and decorate my apartment (and keep it clean)

4. Travel to ancient spiritual places

5. Own a nice home or luxury condo (maybe both)

6. Rent or buy a motorcycle and ride the country side

7. Finish and publish my novel.

I'm surprised to see the hopeless energy. On the one hand, i'm

excited. On the other hand, I feel I'll never get this stuff done.

So, "hopeless" is the heaviest energy. But, I think it goes deeper.

Why hopeless? When I asked the question, "hopeless" became

"failure" and then I felt incapable - like Frankenstein's Igor. He's

'the help' not the genius. I want to be excellent and accomplished.

How would Igor do it? I got it! He has to become an expert - the

master ('yes, master!'). How? I looked it up: Most important steps

seem to be mastering the basics and consistent practice.

7/21/07 - One of the basics I need to master is connecting with

people. Maybe I feel the way I do 'cause I think I'm in this alone.

Your first journey is "Your Personal Renaissance". It consists of twenty-two exercises and master keys that can produce significant shifts in your life. Your journeywork here helps you distinguish your authentic self from your "scripted" self. The scripted self is the you that thinks, says, feels, and does everything it's been conditioned to. It never deviates from the script—not even to experience fulfillment.

When people say, "So tell me about yourself," your scripted self is who you talk about when you tell your story. Maybe the story starts with what you do for a living or the kind of family you come from. Whatever the details, the more of them people know, the more they think they know you. But the story of yourself and the authentic reality of yourself are two completely different things. Very few people know themselves outside of the story they tell. This journey propels you to get to know yourself outside of your story. It is only by moving beyond the script of your life story that you are free to move toward your destiny

Journey 1

Your Personal
Renaissance

Master Key 1

How does one begin the story of eternity? I say it begins with you. [2]Hope springs eternal and your best hope is always you. [3]You are the source of your own experience. This is the true story of yourself.

Exercise: List and/or make a collage of seven very specific things you hope to do with your life—no matter how big or small.

My Message: ---

My Creative Focus: ---

My Reluctance: ---

My Willingness: --

My Next Step: --

My Deadline: ---

My Results: --

Date:

Negative/Resistance

Positive/Flow

M|B
S|E

M|B
S|E

−

●

+

⸺ Master Key 2 ⸺

You are the stuff that stars are made of. You are a witness to the magic of your true Self because you live this magic every day; do it not reluctantly. [2]Be a participant not just an observer of the world in which you seek to live—that is the secret path to fulfillment. And on this path you will learn, while others seek pointlessly to be on top of the world, that a far higher vantage point can be attained. [3]Recognize that your vision is a factor of your perspective. [4]Let your intuition and inner wisdom shine through, and you will not have to rely upon the glitter of gold to light your way.

Exercise: Note the average weekly time spent on activities that have a direct impact on creating the life that you want. Increase it by 15-100%.

My Message: ⸺⸺⸺⸺⸺⸺⸺⸺⸺⸺⸺⸺⸺⸺

My Creative Focus: ⸺⸺⸺⸺⸺⸺⸺⸺⸺⸺⸺⸺

My Reluctance: ⸺⸺⸺⸺⸺⸺⸺⸺⸺⸺⸺⸺⸺

My Willingness: ⸺⸺⸺⸺⸺⸺⸺⸺⸺⸺⸺⸺⸺

My Next Step: ⸺⸺⸺⸺⸺⸺⸺⸺⸺⸺⸺⸺⸺

My Deadline: ⸺⸺⸺⸺⸺⸺⸺⸺⸺⸺⸺⸺⸺

My Results: ⸺⸺⸺⸺⸺⸺⸺⸺⸺⸺⸺⸺⸺

Date: Note to Self

Negative/Resistance   Positive/Flow

M B   M B
S E   S E

⊖━━━━━━━━━━━━━━━●━━━━━━━━━━━━━━━⊕

Master Key 3

Know that you cannot escape the bottom by ascending to the top, for your top is defined by the existence of a bottom. It is a far better choice to make your foundation free, clear, sturdy, and strong. [2]You will not escape a mess by simply leaving it wherever it may lay. You escape it only by cleaning it up. [3]And in this vein, understand the masks you wear do not enhance your character; like a mess they cover up the foundation underneath, upon which your whole life is built. They come between you and others and hide you both from one another. [4]Be your true Self at all times. Have unwavering faith that that is all you ever need to be.

Exercise: List the "messes" in your life. How are choices and relationships affected by efforts to hide or work around them? Clear them up.

My Message: --

My Creative Focus: ---

My Reluctance: --

My Willingness: ---

My Next Step: ---

My Deadline: --

My Results: ---

Date:

Negative/Resistance

Positive/Flow

M B
S E

M B
S E

⊖ ———————— ● ———————— ⊕

Master Key 4

The center of the Universe is where you stand. And know you have nothing of value except what is left when you stand alone. [2]Lift the canopy from your personal world and allow a freedom bird to blossom from the cosmic flower that is you. [3]Be free as a puff of smoke following the wind, passing through the fabric of time and space, leaving its essence behind yet holding on to nothing. [4]Hear the Universe around you pulsing within you all the time. Know the sound of joy is nowhere if not in you. Fear not the divine whispers from within. Listen to the innermost Self for it is the wise one who loves you.

Exercise: What do you and others see as your greatest assets or talents? Collect fifteen ideas for using them to create more freedom in your life.

My Message: ---

My Creative Focus: ---

My Reluctance: ---

My Willingness: --

My Next Step: --

My Deadline: ---

My Results: --

Date: Note to Self

Negative/Resistance   Positive/Flow

M B   M B
S E   S E

⊖ ———————————————— ● ———————————————— ⊕

Master Key 5

How will you continue the story of yourself? I say love thyself a little bit more each day. Use your inner power daily in brand-new ways. [2]The process of illumination is gradual and ongoing. Healing is gradual and ongoing. Your growth is gradual and ongoing. Awareness is gradual and ever-expanding. [3]Allow the time and space that is needed for all things to happen, for all things happen in the Divine Right Order anyway. [4]If you should stand fearful in the face of uncertainty, know that one thing is certain: the purpose of whatever happens next is to bring you closer to your innermost Self.

Exercise: List your five greatest fears. Ask a friend or elder how they handled similar fears. Prepare, practice, or train to overcome yours.

My Message: --

My Creative Focus: ---

My Reluctance: --

My Willingness: ---

My Next Step: ---

My Deadline: --

My Results: --

Negative/Resistance

Positive/Flow

M B
S E

M B
S E

⊖ ● ⊕

Master Key 6

You are likened to a well of water rising to the top as stones are placed deep within it. Every stone is a step you have taken—intentioned or not—toward your own enlightenment. Let your essence rise up to the brim and flow out from the vessel that is your body and your mind.

Exercise: What do you see in yourself or for yourself now that you didn't see before? "Show-and-Tell" it through a form of art.

My Message: --

My Creative Focus: ---

My Reluctance: ---

My Willingness: --

My Next Step: --

My Deadline: ---

My Results: --

Date:

Negative/Resistance

Positive/Flow

M B
S E

M B
S E

$-$ ⊙ $+$

Master Key 7

Seek the Inner Light. [2]And if you should grow fearful thinking, Illumination requires too great a sacrifice, I tell you illumination demands no sacrifice, only an exchange that leaves you in possession of something infinitely greater than what you had to offer. [3]Spiritual growth and depth bring freedom from the perceived limitations of human existence. [4]Worry not about who you used to be or who you have always been. Fill that space instead with excitement about who you are becoming. [5]You are your own authority, your own creator of circumstance. Never abdicate your throne.

Exercise: Pick a talent or skill you would like to develop over the next year and eventually master. Seek formal or informal instruction.

My Message: --

My Creative Focus: --

My Reluctance: --

My Willingness: --

My Next Step: --

My Deadline: --

My Results: --

Negative/Resistance

Positive/Flow

M B
S E

M B
S E

⊖————————————————●————————————————⊕

_____

_____

_____

_____

_____

_____

_____

_____

_____

_____

_____

_____

_____

_____

_____

_____

_____

_____

_____

_____

_____

‹‹‹›› Master Key 8 ‹‹‹››

Y ou are the dreamer and the dreamed. But a dream not shared is like a rainbow unseen. [2]Mastery of inner strength over outer forces is essential to joyful living and manifesting a dream. [3]And when you experience success, do not clench it as though you will never see it again. Enjoy it and then let it go to make room for the next one.

Exercise: Share or demonstrate any of your talents or skills through a public forum, such as a talk, performance, class, or article.

My Message: ---

My Creative Focus: --

My Reluctance: --

My Willingness: ---

My Next Step: --

My Deadline: ---

My Results: --

Date:

Negative/Resistance

M | B
S | E

M | B
S | E

Positive/Flow

⊖━━━━━━━━━━━━━━━━━●━━━━━━━━━━━━━━━━━⊕

_____

_____

_____

_____

_____

_____

_____

_____

_____

_____

_____

_____

_____

_____

_____

_____

_____

_____

_____

_____

_____

_____

_____

_____

_____

Master Key 9

Action and inaction are both forces that shape reality. In what shape is your reality? [2]They say a bird in the hand is worth two in the bush. What bird is in your hand? Are you clutching it to death in fear of losing it or are you giving it the gentle support it needs to grow? [3]To nurture is not to force something to be what it should, but to allow it to be what it is. Nurture yourself. Let go of life as you know it to experience life as it is. Give yourself the proper attention, time, and space to grow. [4]Your destiny is to move forward, not around in circles. But know this: At times the desire to move forward is best fulfilled by standing still.

Exercise: Recall three or more life-changing events (for better or worse) that occurred because you did not act. How would you respond now?

My Message: --

My Creative Focus: ---

My Reluctance: --

My Willingness: ---

My Next Step: ---

My Deadline: --

My Results: ---

Date:

Negative/Resistance

M B
S E

M B
S E

Positive/Flow

⊖ ——————————— ● ——————————— ⊕

_____
_____
_____
_____
_____
_____
_____
_____
_____
_____
_____
_____
_____
_____
_____
_____
_____
_____
_____
_____
_____
_____
_____
_____
_____

Master Key 10

I ask you, how long will you tell the story of yourself? I say a thing need not last forever to be worthwhile. It need only be worthwhile while it lasts. Time consists only of the moment; the moment is all there is. To get anything out of it you must first be in it. [2]You can never be anywhere other than Here, but Here can always expand. [3]The spot on which you stand is always the most important part of the path you are walking.

Exercise: Randomly throughout the day, jot down your thoughts. How often are you in the past, future or fantasy land? Focus on the present.

My Message: --

My Creative Focus: --

My Reluctance: ---

My Willingness: --

My Next Step: --

My Deadline: --
My Results: --

Date:

Negative/Resistance

M B
S E

M B
S E

Positive/Flow

⊖ ● ⊕

Master Key 11

The biggest error made on the quest for knowledge and power is overlooking the knowledge and power you already have acquired. [2]If you think you must have it all, you will always have nothing. [3]Power without focus is powerless. Knowledge without wisdom is trivia. [4]The smallest dose of concentration and purpose can turn the tiniest spark into a universe of glory.

Exercise: Make a list or scrapbook of your top fifty life achievements—no matter how small or how long ago.

My Message: ---

My Creative Focus: --

My Reluctance: --

My Willingness: ---

My Next Step: --

My Deadline: ---

My Results: --

Date: Note to Self

Negative/Resistance   Positive/Flow

M B   M B
S E   S E

⊖━━━━━━━━━━━━━━━━●━━━━━━━━━━━━━━━━⊕

_____

_____

_____

_____

_____

_____

_____

_____

_____

_____

_____

_____

_____

_____

_____

_____

_____

_____

_____

_____

_____

_____

_____

⸺ Master Key 12 ⸺

True, lasting power lies with the current, not against it. Go with the inner flow of power. [2]All answers, all solutions, all reasons can be sought, found, and understood with the power whose source is your very soul.

Exercise: What natural "gifts" do you most easily draw upon to create change for yourself and others? How consistently do you use them?

My Message: ⸺⸺⸺⸺⸺⸺⸺⸺⸺⸺⸺⸺⸺⸺⸺⸺⸺⸺⸺

⸺⸺⸺⸺⸺⸺⸺⸺⸺⸺⸺⸺⸺⸺⸺⸺⸺⸺⸺⸺⸺⸺

My Creative Focus: ⸺⸺⸺⸺⸺⸺⸺⸺⸺⸺⸺⸺⸺⸺⸺⸺⸺

⸺⸺⸺⸺⸺⸺⸺⸺⸺⸺⸺⸺⸺⸺⸺⸺⸺⸺⸺⸺⸺⸺

My Reluctance: ⸺⸺⸺⸺⸺⸺⸺⸺⸺⸺⸺⸺⸺⸺⸺⸺⸺⸺

⸺⸺⸺⸺⸺⸺⸺⸺⸺⸺⸺⸺⸺⸺⸺⸺⸺⸺⸺⸺⸺⸺

My Willingness: ⸺⸺⸺⸺⸺⸺⸺⸺⸺⸺⸺⸺⸺⸺⸺⸺⸺⸺

⸺⸺⸺⸺⸺⸺⸺⸺⸺⸺⸺⸺⸺⸺⸺⸺⸺⸺⸺⸺⸺⸺

My Next Step: ⸺⸺⸺⸺⸺⸺⸺⸺⸺⸺⸺⸺⸺⸺⸺⸺⸺⸺

⸺⸺⸺⸺⸺⸺⸺⸺⸺⸺⸺⸺⸺⸺⸺⸺⸺⸺⸺⸺⸺⸺

My Deadline: ⸺⸺⸺⸺⸺⸺⸺⸺⸺⸺⸺⸺⸺⸺⸺⸺⸺⸺⸺

My Results: ⸺⸺⸺⸺⸺⸺⸺⸺⸺⸺⸺⸺⸺⸺⸺⸺⸺⸺⸺

⸺⸺⸺⸺⸺⸺⸺⸺⸺⸺⸺⸺⸺⸺⸺⸺⸺⸺⸺⸺⸺⸺

Date: Note to Self

Negative/Resistance   Positive/Flow

                    M | B   M | B
                    S | E   S | E

⊖━━━━━━━━━━━━━━━━━━●━━━━━━━━━━━━━━━━━━⊕

~ 51 ~

Master Key 13

With whom will you share the story of yourself? [2]I say the magic of love and relationships lies in their power to magnify the innermost Self and make each of you better, stronger, and wiser than you were before. Anything less is an abuse of power. [3]What is innermost is always present whether you show it or not. [4]Be aware of how you touch others and be not afraid to let others touch you. [5]There is a time to shield oneself and a time to lay oneself bare. Which time is it for you?

Exercise: Who are you close to? How close are you really? Think of ways to get closer. Initiate closeness with a call or other invitation.

My Message: ---

My Creative Focus: --

My Reluctance: ---

My Willingness: --

My Next Step: --

My Deadline: ---

My Results: --

Date:

Note to Self

Negative/Resistance

Positive/Flow

M B
S E

M B
S E

⊖ ———————————————— ● ———————————————— ⊕

Master Key 14

You must watch the words you use and the hidden messages lodged between them. Think not only of what you want to say but also why you want to say it. [2]At times we are so driven to action, so determined to initiate change that we learn too late that the force of rebellion is not always the force we need. [3]A kind, inspiring word can travel farther and gather more power than one could ever expect.

Exercise: For at least three days, do not gossip or speak negatively to anyone or of anyone in their absence.

My Message: --

My Creative Focus: --

My Reluctance: --

My Willingness: ---

My Next Step: ---

My Deadline: --

My Results: ---

Date:

Negative/Resistance

M|B
S|E

M|B
S|E

Positive/Flow

⊖━━━━━━━━━━━●━━━━━━━━━━━⊕

Master Key 15

Kindness is its own reward because when it is done for kindness' sake, when it is done because it is the right thing to do, when it is given freely and not on loan with expectation of acknowledgement or reward, it generates a pure force in divine power. Do kindness for no other reason than kindness in the world be done.

Exercise: Perform ten anonymous acts of kindness. Tell no one of your work or intentions, especially those whose approval you crave.

My Message: ---

My Creative Focus: --

My Reluctance: --

My Willingness: ---

My Next Step: ---

My Deadline: --

My Results: ---

Date:

Negative/Resistance

M B
S E

M B
S E

Positive/Flow

−   ●   +

Master Key 16

What do you think of the story of yourself? I say your thought has power. The thought you think is you—an offspring of your innermost Self. ²A thought lives, it moves, it breathes, it builds. What are you building? With whom do you build it? And to whose specifications will it be built? ³The most intense power is that which is focused. The most creative force is that which maintains its intensity through to completion. The most useful energy is that which allows free expression of the innermost Self.

Exercise: List what you think, worry, or fantasize about most. Put a star next to any item you are addressing with consistent, constructive action.

My Message: --

My Creative Focus: ---

My Reluctance: ---

My Willingness: --

My Next Step: --

My Deadline: ---

My Results: --

Date: Note to Self

Negative/Resistance

M B
S E

M B
S E

Positive/Flow

⊖━━━━━━━━━━━●━━━━━━━━━━━⊕

⚮ Master Key 17 ⚮

Inner Wisdom and Knowing are beyond thinking, beyond the reasoning of the mind. They are beyond opinion, beyond judgment, beyond your ability to assess. [2]It is when you are not thinking that you feel Inner Wisdom come through. [3]Advancement comes often by doing the unthinkable and entering into the Unknown.

Exercise: When opportunity or inspiration to be spontaneous arises, seize it. Be aware of your internal reactions to each situation.

My Message: --

My Creative Focus: ---

My Reluctance: ---

My Willingness: --

My Next Step: --

My Deadline: ---

My Results: --

Date:

Negative/Resistance

M B
S E

M B
S E

Positive/Flow

$\ominus$ ———————————— $\bullet$ ———————————— $\oplus$

Master Key 18

Desire drives us to action. Yet manifestation cannot happen if you depend on the method by which the outcome takes place; it is then that you forget you have the power to make a way out of no way at all. [2]Do not labor the mind too greatly with the task of understanding or the task of finding the way. It is the perception of the innermost Self that guides you.

Exercise: Take your most "impossible" idea or elusive dream to a supportive group for help in brainstorming ways to manifest it.

My Message: --

My Creative Focus: --

My Reluctance: --

My Willingness: --

My Next Step: --

My Deadline: --

My Results: --

Date:

Negative/Resistance

Positive/Flow

M B
S E

M B
S E

$-$

$+$

Master Key 19

Do you know the story of yourself never ends? I say it is a living thing with everlasting life. ²Perhaps it is a thing written time and time again, every line and the stories between them growing greater in their depth. ³Perhaps it is a thing told from one mind to the next, its details changing with every revelation. ⁴Perhaps it is a thing imagined, a thing alive only in the mind of That Which Cannot Be Named.

Exercise: List ten things you've done (positive or negative) that have, or will have, an ever-present effect on the lives of others.

My Message: --

My Creative Focus: --

My Reluctance: --

My Willingness: ---

My Next Step: ---

My Deadline: --

My Results: --

Date:

Negative/Resistance

Positive/Flow

M B
S E

M B
S E

− ● +

Master Key 20

That which has no face, That which has no form, That which only is and is not, cannot be explained—it defies explanation. It cannot be taught—its totality is unknowable. [2]It can be experienced and still never completely understood. [3]It is what it is and it is what you think it is not, and so it is also what you have never dreamt.

Exercise: Based solely on your experience (not learned philosophy or doctrine), what do you understand about the source of your existence?

My Message: --

My Creative Focus: --

My Reluctance: --

My Willingness: ---

My Next Step: ---

My Deadline: --

My Results: ---

Negative/Resistance

Positive/Flow

M B
S E

M B
S E

⚊ Master Key 21 ⚊

That which some call God; That which some call the Universe, That which some call Infinity, the Great Spirit, the Source, the One, the Way; That which some call the All and the Nothing; That which some call the Void is your greatest potential and your purest power. [2]And so when you do the will of the Way, you act not the part of a slave to a master; you do your own highest good.

Exercise: What's the best that can be done to reach your greatest potential? Is that different from what you're actually doing?

My Message: ---

My Creative Focus: ---

My Reluctance: ---

My Willingness: --

My Next Step: --

My Deadline: ---

My Results: --

Negative/Resistance

Positive/Flow

M B
S E

M B
S E

⊖ ————————————— ● ————————————— ⊕

━ Master Key 22 ━

How does one begin the story of eternity? I say it begins with you.

Exercise: Write a short autobiography of your dream life. Add photos or video, using props and costumes as needed. Be creative. Bring it to life.

My Message: --

My Creative Focus: ---

My Reluctance: --

My Willingness: --

My Next Step: ---

My Deadline: --

My Results: ---

Negative/Resistance

Positive/Flow

M B
S E

M B
S E

−

+

"What were you thinking?" Have you ever asked anyone that? Has anyone ever asked you that in the wake of some disaster that could have been foreseen and avoided? Right now there are millions of people who are consciously or unconsciously moving away from their goals in life and waiting for the end—the end of the year, the end of their career, the end of their marriage, the end of the road, the end of some particular chapter in their story, the end of their life—before doing anything to change their life's direction. Are you one of those people? Are you so distracted by your outer achievements or setbacks that you remain oblivious to what's happening within and around you as you obsess over them? Although hindsight may sometimes be 20/20, the truth is, by the time you look back, what's done is done. If, however, you can gain insight into the present moment, you will enjoy the creative power and immediate satisfaction of making the most of it. Your journeywork through "Your Goal in Life" can lead to important insights about your life goals, choices, and what they can create for you right now.

Choices make the world go 'round because they commit our thoughts, energy, and attention in one direction or the other. Every choice you make—to lie, to tell the truth, to go, to stay, to apologize, to keep quiet, to smile, to frown, to sleep, to stay awake, to punish, to forgive—commits your life to one direction or another. It is in the choosing that life really happens. While some choices may be difficult or unpleasant, if you are deliberate about making appropriate choices in the moment, then you can also be at peace in the moment with how your life is going. The exercise and master key for this journey empowers you to choose authentic goals that bring immediate peace to your life.

Your Goal in Life

Master Key 23

Perhaps your goal is to look back on your life and say, "I am pleased with what I have done." Perhaps your goal is to look back on your year and say, "I am pleased with what I have done." Or perhaps your goal is to look back on your month, your week, your day, and say, "I am pleased with what I have done." Know the real goal is to be in the moment and say, "I am at peace with what I am choosing."

Exercise: Periodically, throughout the day, ask yourself if you are at peace with whatever you are choosing to do or not do.

My Message: --

My Creative Focus: --

My Reluctance: --

My Willingness: --

My Next Step: ---

My Deadline: --

My Results: --

Date: Note to Self

Negative/Resistance   Positive/Flow

                    M B   M B
                    S E   S E

⊖━━━━━━━━━━━━━━━●━━━━━━━━━━━━━━━⊕

Do you know the story of The Little Engine That Could? A train hauling toys and other things to boys and girls anxiously awaiting on the other side of a mountain suddenly breaks down. Several big trains pass by offering one excuse after another for not stopping to help. Finally, along comes the Little Engine. Small though it was, and seemingly incapable of pulling the broken-down train full of toys over the mountain, the Little Engine chooses to call upon its inner strength rather than be hindered by its apparent limitations. "I think I can, I think I can, I think I can," it tells itself as it struggles to the mountaintop. As it finally reaches the peak and starts to run effortlessly down the other side toward its destination, the Little Engine praises itself, "I knew I could, I knew I could, I knew I could." The journey to "Your Essential Nature" is the journey of The Little Spirit That Could—the spirit that could envision its potential and rise to a challenge; that could think beyond its apparent limitations and dare to achieve the impossible; that could motivate itself to reach the mountaintop and run toward its destiny. That spirit, of course, is you.

No matter how much you ignore or deny the inner strength of your spirit, it is still there within you anyway. When you resist it, you merely weaken your ability to use it effectively and favorably in your life. The exercise and master key for this journey will help open you up to your true potential for greatness—if you let it!

Journey III

Your Essential
Nature

Master Key 24

You are a powerful, magical being. Be it! [2]Your mind is a door to the Universe. Open it! [3]Your true Self resides in your heart. Express it! [4]Each moment is a chance to be free. Take it!

Exercise: Spend time in nature and contemplate your relationship to the universe of life. Offer a gift that enhances your relationship.

My Message: --

My Creative Focus: ---

My Reluctance: --

My Willingness: ---

My Next Step: ---

My Deadline: --

My Results: ---

Date: Note to Self

Negative/Resistance   Positive/Flow

M|B   M|B
S|E   S|E

⊖━━━━━━━━━━●━━━━━━━━━━⊕

_____
_____
_____
_____
_____
_____
_____
_____
_____
_____
_____
_____
_____
_____
_____
_____
_____
_____
_____
_____
_____
_____
_____
_____
_____

The truth hurts. That's what we've been told. So when doubt enters your mind about why someone did what they did, or why this thing or that did or did not happen for you, the tendency is to gravitate toward ignorant bliss rather than investigate the truth. You gravitate toward ignorance when you're afraid of what you might learn if you start asking serious questions. Knowledge of the truth often breeds responsibility.

You gravitate toward ignorance when you're afraid of what you may have to confront—what you'll have to be responsible for—once the truth is revealed. You run from the truth when you're terrified it will make a negative or humiliating statement about you. Contrary to popular belief, truth does not hurt. What hurts is the judgment you make about yourself and others based on the truth. Judgments perpetuate doubt, fear, and confusion. They do nothing to transform the situation. Judgments cloud the path to destiny and authentic self-fulfillment. Your journeywork in "Conquering the Mind of Doubt" helps to clear the cloud.

Journey IV

Conquering the Mind of Doubt

Master Key 25

In the mind of doubt lies fear—the enemy of your true Self. And there it plants its backward seed that unravels you from deep within. [2]You embrace doubt only when you are reluctant to know the truth for sure. [3]The truth is not a judgment; truth is a guiding light. When in doubt, seek the truth.

Exercise: What is your greatest doubt about yourself or your future? Use the wisdom above to remove all doubt.

My Message: --

My Creative Focus: --

My Reluctance: --

My Willingness: --

My Next Step: ---

My Deadline: --

My Results: ---

Date: Note to Self

Negative/Resistance

M B   M B
S E   S E

Positive/Flow

⊖━━━━━━━━━━●━━━━━━━━━━⊕

Whatever personal gain you may acquire in life, how profitable is it really if you overtax your mind, body, and emotions in the process of attaining it? If you invest time, money, and effort into things that are fleeting and insignificant, you will find the grandness of your life escaping you. You will find yourself losing hope, faith, energy, vitality, health, clarity, opportunity, respect, joy, support, friendship, love, and attention. You will find yourself losing your ground, losing your grip, losing your balance—losing yourself. To lose sight of what matters is to suffer quite a loss indeed.

Many people are running on empty—some without even knowing it—because the outer trappings and distractions of the material world temporarily mask the depletion of their inner resources. To journey successfully across "Your Energetic Bottom Line" is to replenish and multiply the authentic value of your life. The exercises and master keys for this journey help you inventory and wisely invest your vital energy and authentic power.

Your Energetic Bottom Line

Master Key 26

Consider for a moment that you are an equation—the sum of what you think, say, feel and do. [2]Every thought, every word, every deed, every inner experience is an investment. Are you living profitably or do you operate at a loss?

Exercise: In your interactions with others, observe your effect on each other's equation. What is the value? Can you increase it?

My Message: --

My Creative Focus: ---

My Reluctance: ---

My Willingness: --

My Next Step: --

My Deadline: ---

My Results: --

Date:

Negative/Resistance

Positive/Flow

M B
S E

M B
S E

⊖ ━━━━━━━━━━━━━━━━━━━━━ ⬤ ━━━━━━━━━━━━━━━━━━━━━ ⊕

Master Key 27

It takes energy to make energy, but how much energy are you making? [2]It is not your imagination that some things make you feel alive. And it is not your imagination that some things make you feel spent. Every use of energy, every application of effort, causes an effect. You affect yourself each and every day. Consider the effect you are causing. [3]Consider your energetic bottom line.

Exercise: For a week, note if you are energized or drained by day's end. Assess all activities, including eating. Mark each with a "+" or "-."

My Message: --

My Creative Focus: --

My Reluctance: --

My Willingness: ---

My Next Step: ---

My Deadline: --

My Results: ---

Date: Note to Self

Negative/Resistance   Positive/Flow

M B   M B
S E   S E

⊖ ——————————— ● ——————————— ⊕

_____
_____
_____
_____
_____
_____
_____
_____
_____
_____
_____
_____
_____
_____
_____
_____
_____
_____
_____
_____
_____
_____
_____

Relationships with others have great impact on your sense of self. Relationships can offer an external view of your innermost thoughts about yourself—who you are, who you hope to be, who you're ready to be, who you're afraid to be, and what you're willing or unwilling to do about it. The responses, reactions, and interactions you experience in your outer relationships directly reflect the relationship issues you have with your innermost Self. Sometimes you unconsciously use relationships to distract you from the inner reality that needs attention. When you relate soul-to-soul rather than ego-to-ego, you can recognize and seize opportunities for mutual growth. Your journeywork in "Relationships" intensifies your collaborative and creative power to reach your destiny.

What you see in others, what attracts, repels, empowers or disempowers you when you relate to others, offers important insight into your own capacity for self-love and nurturing. True self-love and self-fulfillment are interdependent. The exercises and master keys for this journey help you distinguish true, soul-based love from that which passes for love in the ego's eyes.

Journey VI

Relationships

⸺ Master Key 28 ⸺

What is a relationship? For some, a relationship is defined by past experiences; realize experience does not always constitute understanding. [2]For others, a relationship is a habit; it may be time to change your ways. [3]For those who don't know better, a relationship is a chore—the endless task of projecting and aspiring to unmeetable expectations. Be joyful in knowing a relationship is more glorious than that.

Exercise: List at least three glorious moments from your most important relationships, or show them through pictures, music, or poetry.

My Message: --

My Creative Focus: ---

My Reluctance: ---

My Willingness: --

My Next Step: --

My Deadline: ---

My Results: --

Date: _____ Note to Self

Negative/Resistance

| | M | B | | | M | B |
| | S | E | | | S | E |

Positive/Flow

⊖━━━━━━━━━━●━━━━━━━━━━⊕

~~~~~~
~~~~~~
~~~~~~
~~~~~~
~~~~~~
~~~~~~
~~~~~~
~~~~~~
~~~~~~
~~~~~~
~~~~~~
~~~~~~
~~~~~~
~~~~~~
~~~~~~
~~~~~~
~~~~~~
~~~~~~
~~~~~~
~~~~~~

⟡ Master Key 29 ⟡

A relationship is a state of connectedness. [2]How you connect with others will not differ greatly from the way you
connect with yourself. [3]Like dots, your mind will connect to
form some pattern and picture in the world. If you share a
common vision, a breathtaking picture it will be.

Exercise: Compare what you like most and least about your important
relationships with what you like most and least about yourself.

My Message: --

My Creative Focus: ---

My Reluctance: ---

My Willingness: --

My Next Step: --

My Deadline: ---

My Results: --

Date:

Note to Self

Negative/Resistance

Positive/Flow

M B
S E

M B
S E

─○─────────────────────●─────────────────────⊕

Master Key 30

Do not become blind and think romantic relationships are the only ones that matter. [2]But if you do seek love, know that it is ever abundant; you cannot run out. [3]To find love, demonstrate it. Be the love of your own life, and you will never want for companionship.

Exercise: How would your life be different with the ideal lover, friends, or family? Don't wait for the ideal—become it!.

My Message: --

My Creative Focus: ---

My Reluctance: ---

My Willingness: --

My Next Step: --

My Deadline: ---

My Results: --

Date: Note to Self

Negative/Resistance | M B / S E | | M B / S E | Positive/Flow

$\ominus$ ———————————— $\bullet$ ———————————— $\oplus$

Master Key 31

The unconscious lover often seeks to mend the broken relationship with the self through relationships with others. You cannot heal yourself this way. [2]If in your search for love you seek really to fulfill your needs, know this: needs change. [3]Seek instead a partner who will help you fulfill yourself. As your needs change, the bond between you will remain unbroken.

Exercise: List what you want most from a partner. Which of those do you withhold from yourself or others? Open up. Learn to improve.

My Message: --

My Creative Focus: --

My Reluctance: --

My Willingness: ---

My Next Step: ---

My Deadline: --

My Results: ---

Date: Note to Self

Negative/Resistance   Positive/Flow

M B   M B
S E   S E

⊖━━━━━━━━━●━━━━━━━━━⊕

Master Key 32

¹f you desire a good relationship, focus on what you intend to contribute rather than what you expect to gain. ²If you desire commitment, commit to yourself first—a good relationship will uphold the vow you make to self.

Exercise: List ten "gifts" or contributions you are ready, able, and willing to make to a relationship. Offer them.

My Message: --

My Creative Focus: --

My Reluctance: --

My Willingness: ---

My Next Step: --

My Deadline: ---

My Results: --

Date: Note to Self

Negative/Resistance   Positive/Flow

              M B   M B
              S E   S E

⊖━━━━━━━━━━━━━━━━━●━━━━━━━━━━━━━━━━━⊕

_____
_____
_____
_____
_____
_____
_____
_____
_____
_____
_____
_____
_____
_____
_____
_____
_____
_____
_____
_____
_____
_____
_____

Master Key 33

They say love conquers all. But it is not the nature of love to conquer anything. What love does is endure while all else fades away. ²So never fall in love—rise in it always.

Exercise: Pick any ten people you love. Give them each something once a month (tangible or intangible) to nurture them and help them "rise."

My Message: --

My Creative Focus: ---

My Reluctance: --

My Willingness: ---

My Next Step: ---

My Deadline: --

My Results: ---

Date:

Negative/Resistance

Positive/Flow

M B
S E

M B
S E

−

+

Ego is the fabricated, surface identity we come to erroneously accept as Self. Over time it becomes a hardened shell of conditioned responses and views, and seeks endlessly to justify itself and remain unchanged. The ego is always on the lookout for a threat—some potential breach of inner security. When in doubt, ego assumes the worst and goes on the defensive to resist, protect, deny, enforce, judge, distract, isolate, divide, and conquer. A threatened ego is the number one cause of inner and outer conflict and stress. Your journeywork for "Diminishing Conflict, Ego & Stress" in your life will help you develop a new approach for dealing with common experiences in which you are most likely to get caught up in your ego and lose sight of yourself, what's real, what matters, and what works.

The ego is not a creative problem solver. It always does whatever it has always done. Ego leads to rigor mortis of the mind and emotions, eventually rendering you inflexible in your thoughts, perception, approach, character, and courses of action. When you diminish ego, you increase exponentially your identification with authentic Self and your ability to consciously interact with what's happening within and around you. The less ego you have, the easier it is to maintain equilibrium while life happens. The exercises and master keys help to prevent you from losing hold of yourself when the pressure is on. They can help you connect with the right choices and action that will bring peace, healing, resolution, and fulfillment in the heat of the moment.

Diminishing Conflict, Ego & Stress

Master Key 34

Stop. Breathe. Relax. Laugh. Play.

Exercise: What tension do you need to relax in your mind, body, attitude or life? Unwind. Let go your ego. Stretch the body, heart and mind.

My Message: --

My Creative Focus: --

My Reluctance: --

My Willingness: --

My Next Step: ---

My Deadline: --

My Results: --

Date:

Negative/Resistance

Positive/Flow

M B
S E

M B
S E

$\ominus$ ———————————————— $\bullet$ ———————————————— $\oplus$

— Master Key 35 —

When the winds of change blow, bend like a reed. Let the mind flex. Let the dream evolve. For when the winds die down, the reed is still left standing.

Exercise: Recall a recent situation in which you resisted change. What were you really resisting? Where/how do you need to be more flexible?

My Message: --

My Creative Focus: --

My Reluctance: --

My Willingness: ---

My Next Step: ---

My Deadline: --

My Results: ---

Date: Note to Self

MB   MB
SE   SE

$\ominus$ ————————————————————— $\bullet$ —————————————————————— $\oplus$

_____
_____
_____
_____
_____
_____
_____
_____
_____
_____
_____
_____
_____
_____
_____
_____
_____
_____
_____
_____
_____
_____
_____
_____

Master Key 36

There is Who You Are and there is What Happens to You, and there is also your decision about how what happens affects Who You Are.

Exercise: List five positive traits or talents you once had but no longer show. When/how/why did you "bury" them? Reclaim at least one.

My Message: --

My Creative Focus: --

My Reluctance: --

My Willingness: ---

My Next Step: ---

My Deadline: --

My Results: ---

Date:

Note to Self

Negative/Resistance

Positive/Flow

M B
S E

M B
S E

─○──────────────●──────────────⊕─

Master Key 37

An opinion is not the truth. [2]A belief is not knowledge. [3]Knowledge is not understanding. [4]An interpretation is not a fact. [5]A perspective is not the big picture. [6]How you felt is not what happened. [7]An emotional reaction is not a conscious response. [8]An excuse is not a reason. A reason is not a purpose. [9]A poor decision is not the same as a mistake. [10]Convenience is not a necessity. [11]Change is not the same as progress.

Exercise: Observe your negative internal and external reactions to people or events. Contemplate the relevance of any of the above verses.

My Message: --

My Creative Focus: --

My Reluctance: --

My Willingness: ---

My Next Step: ---

My Deadline: --

My Results: ---

Date: Note to Self

Negative/Resistance

M B   M B
S E   S E

Positive/Flow

⊖ ————————————●———————————— ⊕

Master Key 38

Suns shine. That is what they do until they are suns no more. And likewise, transgressors transgress. That is what they do until they are transgressors no more. All things behave according to their nature, not according to you. ²So if you desire to forgive the sun for shining, if you desire to forgive a transgressor for transgressing, if you want to forgive anything at all, first acknowledge its nature. To forgive is not to pardon but to set yourself free from your own false expectations.

Exercise: What grudges, anger or hurt are you holding—and for how long? What decisions have you made (or not made) because of them?

My Message: --

My Creative Focus: ---

My Reluctance: ---

My Willingness: --

My Next Step: --

My Deadline: ---

My Results: --

Negative/Resistance

Positive/Flow

M B
S E

M B
S E

⊖——————————————●——————————————⊕

⸺ Master Key 39 ⸺

Never presume that one is "guilty" of falling short of your expectations. [2]And never presume that one is "guilty" of living up to your expectations. [3]Better yet, suspend your expectations. Presume the truth has yet to be revealed, and let it speak for itself.

Exercise: Mingle at an event, choosing in advance a random group of people to connect with (e.g., people with red hair or silver watches).

My Message: --

My Creative Focus: --

My Reluctance: --

My Willingness: ---

My Next Step: ---

My Deadline: --

My Results: ---

Date:

Negative/Resistance

| | M | B | | | M | B | |
| | S | E | | | S | E | |

Positive/Flow

$\ominus$ ——————————— $\bullet$ ——————————— $\oplus$

_____
_____
_____
_____
_____
_____
_____
_____
_____
_____
_____
_____
_____
_____
_____
_____
_____
_____
_____
_____
_____
_____
_____
_____
_____
_____
_____

~~~ Master Key 40 ~~~

Actions speak louder than words but not necessarily more plainly; actions are subject to interpretation, which is subject to the biases that color the mind. Be clear.

Exercise: When you find yourself or a companion acting out, giving signs, or dropping hints, stop the charade and clear the air.

My Message: ---

My Creative Focus: ---

My Reluctance: --

My Willingness: ---

My Next Step: ---

My Deadline: --

My Results: ---

Date:

Negative/Resistance

M B
S E

M B
S E

Positive/Flow

⊖ ──────────────── ● ──────────────── ⊕

Master Key 41

You are never truly alone. Always there is someone somewhere ready to comfort you or share. Always there is someone somewhere ready to guide you to the next step, or ready to be guided through steps you've already taken. [2]So when you feel alone, reach out, no matter how near or far. Make your True Self available.

Exercise: Volunteer (formally or informally) to help someone out or mentor/tutor them in an area in which you have had some success.

My Message: --

My Creative Focus: ---

My Reluctance: ---

My Willingness: --

My Next Step: --

My Deadline: ---

My Results: --

Date:

Negative/Resistance

Positive/Flow

M B
S E

M B
S E

⊖ ━━━━━━━━━━━━━━●━━━━━━━━━━━━━ ⊕

Master Key 42

Be not afraid to want what you want. And be not afraid to have it.

Exercise: List five things you want and five people who can help you achieve or acquire them. Ask (formally or informally) for what you want.

My Message: --

My Creative Focus: --

My Reluctance: --

My Willingness: --

My Next Step: --

My Deadline: --

My Results: --

Date: Note to Self

Negative/Resistance

M B
S E

M B
S E

Positive/Flow

⊖━━━━━━━━━━━━━━━●━━━━━━━━━━━━━━━⊕

Master Key 43

If you think, *My day will never come*, know your day is already on its way. If you have made an opening in your life and consciousness through which it can reach you, trust it will surely arrive. There is nothing left for you to do but be prepared for when it comes.

Exercise: Of all the things you truly want for yourself, which are you least prepared to handle, and why? Start to prepare.

My Message: --

My Creative Focus: --

My Reluctance: --

My Willingness: ---

My Next Step: ---

My Deadline: --

My Results: ---

Date: Note to Self

Negative/Resistance   Positive/Flow

M B   M B
S E   S E

⊖━━━━━━━━━━━━━●━━━━━━━━━━━━━━━━━━━━━━━⊕

_____
_____
_____
_____
_____
_____
_____
_____
_____
_____
_____
_____
_____
_____
_____
_____
_____
_____
_____
_____
_____
_____
_____
_____
_____

─── **Master Key 44** ───

When inspiration hits, go with it in that moment. If timing is everything, the moment of inspiration is a perfect time to act.

Exercise: Make a note whenever you second-guess yourself. Watch for thought patterns that prevent you from trusting yourself.

My Message: --

My Creative Focus: --

My Reluctance: ---

My Willingness: --

My Next Step: ---

My Deadline: --

My Results: ---

Date:

Note to Self

Negative/Resistance

Positive/Flow

M B
S E

M B
S E

⊖ ————————————●————————————————⊕

Master Key 45

At any given time, the moment requires you to pay attention to what matters most. What matters most is taking the most appropriate action—without hesitation—in relationship to the experience you intend to create. [2]Do what the moment requires, and you can trust that the outcome will be most appropriate, even if not to your liking.

Exercise: Note the time and energy spent thinking negatively about doing an unpleasant task. Stop the negative commentary. See the effect.

My Message: --

My Creative Focus: ---

My Reluctance: ---

My Willingness: --

My Next Step: --

My Deadline: ---

My Results: --

Date:

Negative/Resistance

Positive/Flow

M B
S E

M B
S E

⊖ ●———————————⊕

How much of what goes on in the world happens because of what people do? How much of it happens because of what other people don't do about it? If your individual thoughts create your personal reality (and they do), then understand that our collective thoughts create our social reality. Local and global events are the stage on which our collective thoughts are dramatized. The journey through "Social Consciousness" is an examination of your role in those dramas.

Dependency, complacency, apathy, and fear of rocking the boat are chronic problems in today's society. On this journey, you examine the line between where you end and where you allow society to take your place. You also examine how this affects your ability to live life to the fullest. Individual and collective fulfillment (and dissatisfaction), are reflected back to you through the outer reality. Your journeywork here helps you recognize the extent of your power and take your sense of purpose to a new level.

Journey VIII

Social
Consciousness

Master Key 46

In a society, it is quite a statement of values to consider acts of kindness or service as charity—doing the right thing is the only profitable thing to do. [2]Let not the self become identified with the labels society manufactures; society is not a true authority. [3]The social fabric is woven of threads of many visions. To be a leader in society, create leaders that can consciously weave a pattern together; for though there is power in numbers, there is greater power in focus. [4]So ask not what society can do for you; ask what you should do for yourself.

Exercise: Write to politicians, the media, businesses, organizations, etc., with praise, concern or ideas about their impact on societal matters.

My Message: --

My Creative Focus: ---

My Reluctance: --

My Willingness: ---

My Next Step: ---

My Deadline: --

My Results: ---

Note to Self

Negative/Resistance

Positive/Flow

M B
S E

M B
S E

⊖ ——————————————— ● ——————————————— ⊕

Sometimes a soul's gotta do what a soul's gotta do. The journey through "What Must Be" empowers you to do just that. What you experience up until this point in the process helps you gradually clear your consciousness of things that keep you from authentic self-fulfillment. You will see for yourself, however, that there are times when there simply is no time for anything other than instantaneous transformation. If you intend to live life like you mean it, then you must let yourself arrive at the moment when you stop crawling and choose to take a stand.

The journey through "What Must Be" is an important process in which you begin to mature into your real power. You press onward, go deeper, and make the changes that really matter without making excuses for yourself. You realize there is no excuse for not living the life you are meant because that's what you came here for. This journey offers very simple wisdom, yet it is difficult to stomach if you have grown accustomed to spinning your wheels and going through the motions when it comes to reaching your destiny. The exercise and master key for this journey challenge you to reach an important milestone: to stop stalling and go straight to your destiny.

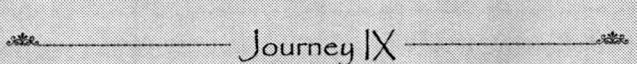

Journey IX

What Must Be

⸻ Master Key 47 ⸻

Do what must be done and do it masterfully without apprehension or vacillation. [2]Say what must be said and say it sincerely without fear or malice. [3]Feel what must be felt and feel it completely without censorship or shame. [4]Listen to what must be heard and listen attentively with openness of heart and mind. [5]Learn what must be known and learn it proficiently in a meaningful context. [6]Question what must be challenged and question it wisely with respect and good intention. [7]Release what must be freed and release it willingly without bitterness or regret.

Exercise: By following which of the directives above can you exact the greatest change in your life right now?

My Message: --

My Creative Focus: --

My Reluctance: --

My Willingness: ---

My Next Step: ---

My Deadline: --

My Results: ---

Date:

Negative/Resistance

Positive/Flow

M B
S E

M B
S E

$-$ ●────────────── $+$

How serious are you about living a fulfilling life from an authentic place of power, while moving consciously toward your destiny? After you have successfully journeyed the previous path of "What Must Be," you will have not only reached an important level of maturation, but you will have also started radiating your unique brilliance with increasing power and consistency. The journey through "Your Responsibility" puts you in touch with a deep and powerful level of inner authority, and urges you to accept full creative and spiritual responsibility for yourself. It is an empowering step that takes guts. In the earlier journey of "Your Essential Nature," you learn that you wield the power of the universe in everything you do. "Your Responsibility" urges you to be ready, able, and willing to wield that power deliberately for the highest good. The exercise and mastery key reveal how you sabotage and cheat yourself out of what is right, and allow you to finally get out of your own way.

Journey X

Your
Responsibility

Master Key 48

The power of the Universe is always on your side. The question is, whose side are you on? Are you for yourself or against yourself? [2]You have no enemy other than yourself, for no matter what is done to you, and no matter what goes on around you, the responsibility to be whole will always rest with you.

Exercise: List the ways in which you tend to work against yourself. For each, create a counterattack and a plan for success.

My Message: --

My Creative Focus: --

My Reluctance: --

My Willingness: --

My Next Step: --

My Deadline: --

My Results: --

Date: Note to Self

Negative/Resistance   Positive/Flow

M B   M B
S E   S E

⊖ ━━━━━━━━━━━━━━ ● ━━━━━━━━━━━━━━ ⊕

_____
_____
_____
_____
_____
_____
_____
_____
_____
_____
_____
_____
_____
_____
_____
_____
_____
_____
_____
_____
_____
_____
_____
_____

Who is in control of your life? Is it you or your mind? The real you is not your mind; neither is it your body nor your ego. When you permit the desires of your false self—the inauthentic self—to overwhelm you, you lose control, you lose momentum, and you lose your capacity to reach your destiny. The desire that manipulates you, the desire over which you relinquish control of yourself and the moment, does not lead to fulfillment. It cannot because only the authentic Self can experience fulfillment. The false self can only be pacified—until its next craving.

Although desire can drive you to action, uncontrolled desire can drive you over the edge. False, uncontrolled desire enslaves you and diverts you away from what is meaningful and real. You gravitate toward false desire when you seek distraction from something you don't want to address. Underneath false desire is an authentic need to fill a void or heal a wound. This journey takes you right into the void, which can only be filled with self-love, nurturing, and truth—things that restore you to the totality of yourself. Authentic self-restoration cannot be wished into being. It can only be brought about through clear intention and consistent focus. The exercise for this final step of the process leads you to a pivotal milestone that helps you fill the void, fulfill your authentic desires, and live the life you are meant.

Desire

·····━━ Master Key 49 ━━·····

L et not a desire control you like a puppet on a string. [2]Examine always if your desire reflects honestly the man or woman you choose to be, and if your choice makes you more in love with your life. [3]When you discover an honest desire for what you do not have, you lack only the resolve to be straight-forwardly proactive. [4]Desire nothing. Intend everything.

Exercise: Name your greatest desire. Replace it with a clear and steadfast intention.

My Message: --

My Creative Focus: --

My Reluctance: --

My Willingness: --

My Next Step: ---

My Deadline: --

My Results: --

Negative/Resistance

Positive/Flow

M B
S E

M B
S E

⊖ ● ⊕

The power of total self-mastery and fulfillment is in your hands.

Your Divine
Self-design

Master Key 50

_____

_____

_____

_____

_____

Exercise: _____

My Message: _____

My Creative Focus: _____

My Reluctance: _____

My Willingness: _____

My Next Step: _____

My Deadline: _____

My Results: _____

Date: Note to Self

Negative/Resistance   Positive/Flow

M B   M B
S E   S E

⊖━━━━━━━━━━━━━━━━━━━●━━━━━━━━━━━━━━━━━━━⊕

_____
_____
_____
_____
_____
_____
_____
_____
_____
_____
_____
_____
_____
_____
_____
_____
_____
_____
_____
_____
_____
_____
_____
_____

- If you're experiencing slow progress or small achievements, take your time with activities for maximum effectiveness. Get some momentum going before moving on.

- If you're stuck, you may be doing too much or too little, or you may have misidentified the energy you need to work with. Don't beat yourself up. Start where you are. Do what you can. Make whatever adjustments you need.

- If you cannot break a negative cycle after completing a workshop, look more deeply into the negative emotional space on your Inner Power Map™. Emotional energy that is out of sync with the new pattern you are trying to adopt is almost always the cause.

- For additional help, go to www.SelfMasteryCamp.com. Courses facilitated by the author are available along with self-coaching courses and discussion forums.

- If you have difficulty grasping a master key or completing an exercise, ask yourself one or more of these soul-searching questions to stimulate your inner wisdom:

    1. What does this say about who I have the potential to be?

    2. How can this improve the way I relate to others or self?

    3. What wounds can I heal by embodying this wisdom?

    4. What responsibility does this encourage me to accept?

    5. What does this wisdom dare me to do?

- Periodically review what you've written. Hindsight can be helpful in fine-tuning your progress and staying on track.

- For insight or guidance about a situation you're facing in the moment, read a verse at random from the book, explore it in meditation or use the index to find a related exercise.

Specializing in personal, professional and spiritual growth, Antonia Martinez, Ph.D. holds a doctorate in metaphysics and is pursuing a second in metaphysical psychology. One of the first producers of metaphysical and holistic Internet talk radio and online learning in the 90's, Dr. Martinez has served an international audience for nearly 15 years. She continues to offer online classes, coaching and professional training via her website, as well as develop custom programs for private groups, businesses and non-profit organizations.

Dr. Martinez draws on a unique blend of eastern, western, indigenous and urban wisdom in her work. After 9/11, she developed a number of corporate programs to help address workplace issues from a holistic perspective. In 2002 she became an ordained metaphysical and shamanic minister. And In 2007, Dr. Martinez created the International Meditation Instructor's Training & Certification program for the Inner Life Society—a nonprofit spiritual organization that promotes conscious living.

Titles by Antonia Martinez, Ph.D.

- *Self-Mastery & Fulfillment Workbook*
- *Self-Determination Journal*
- *Tapping Your Power*
- *The Best You Can*
- *Purpose & Destiny Workshop*

- *7 Spiritual Necessities for Changing Times*
- *Spiritual Sunshine Meditation*
- *Letting Go of Pain, Grief & the Past*

Invite Dr. Martinez to speak at your next event or develop special content or programs for your organization. Learn more about her products and services on her website.

www.AntoniaMartinez.com

Explore new possibilities for your life, career or relationship's direction. Programs based on the *Self-Mastery & Fulfillment Workbook* and related material are excellent tools for individuals as well as for managers, parents, mentors and other leaders to use with their family, group or team.

- **Online Self-Mastery Course**
  An interactive online course and workbook offers bonus self-coaching material from the author. Journal and track your progress online. Share experiences with like-minds.

- **90-day Self-Mastery Camp™**
  Intensify your focus. Achieve more profound results sooner with web-based coaching from the author. Access bonus material and interact with other camp members online.

- **Train-the-Trainer**
  Web-based self-coaching programs and 90-day intensives with the author are available for mentors, managers, parents, educators, etc. Learn to implement, facilitate, and adapt in-house holistic programs that use self-mastery, Inner Power Mapping™ and other personal growth techniques.

- **Self-Mastery Programs for Groups & Organizations**
  Bring holistic programs to your members, staff or students. In-house or online programs as well as informal self-mastery circles based on the workbook or custom lesson plans tailored by Dr. Martinez focus on specific growth objectives or skill development.

For more information, visit www.SelfMasteryCamp.com

Printed in the United States
86038LV00003B/254/A

9 780971 793927